.U52
D576
2017

Walt Disney

The Man Behind The Magic

(A Walt Disney Biography)

AA Christiansen

Metropolitan College of NY
Library - 7th Floor
60 West Street
New York, NY 10006

Copyright © 2017.

All rights reserved. No part of this publication may be reproduced, distributed, or transmitted in any form or by any means, including photocopying, recording, or other electronic or mechanical methods, without the prior written permission of the publisher, except in the case of brief quotations embodied in critical reviews and certain other noncommercial uses permitted by copyright law.

This book is intended for informational and entertainment purposes only. The publisher limits all liability arising from this work to the fullest extent of the law.

Metropolitan College of NY
Library - 7th Floor
60 West Street
New York, NY 10006

Table of Contents

Walt Disney: A Career As Timeless As Mickey Mouse

The Formative Years - His Early Life (1901-1920)

The Start Of A Legend - His Early Career (1920-1928)

Mickey Mouse Is Born – The Academy Awards (1928-1933)

Full Steam Success – The Golden Age Of Animation (1934-1941)

The Second World War And Moving Forward (1941-1950)

New Media – Amusement Parks, Television, And Expanded Interests (1950-1966)

Walt's Failing Health, Cancer, Death, And Beyond (1966 - onward)

The Walt Disney Company (present)

Walt Disney: A Career As Timeless As Mickey Mouse

The legend later known as Walt Disney was born Walter Elias Disney on December 5th in 1901 in Chicago, Illinois and died on December 15th in 1966 in Burbank, California at the age of 65. His work as an American film producer, animator, voice actor, and entrepreneur would lead to a variety of enhancements in the way that we make cartoons and his personal style would touch the world and forever leave his mark. The record for the most Academy Awards as a film producer belongs to him, for a total of fifty-nine nominations and twenty-two wins. Among other honors, he was the recipient of an Emmy Award and two Golden Globe Special Achievement Awards. The National Film Registry hosted by the Library of Congress has many of his films housed in their catalog for preservation as timeless material. With everything from amusement parks to timeless children's classics with his name on them, there are few in the world who do not know of Walt Disney and his successes.

Walt Disney's interest in drawing started early on and he took art classes as a child. This allowed him to explore the hobby under the guidance of a teacher, which would ultimate teach him the value of learning new things. After he turned eighteen, he was able to get a job working as a commercial illustrator for a local company. From there, he took his experience, his talent, and his brother and moved to a bigger city so that they could set up their own studio in California. It was the early 1920s and their shared company name was the Disney Brothers Studio. In 1928, Walt paired with Ub Iwerks and together they would create his first, and arguably most popular and iconic character, Mickey Mouse. In these early years, Walt Disney himself took on the voice acting for his precious creation and is credited for giving the beloved cartoon character the heart and passion that made the world fall in love with him.

As the years went by, the studio's experience and opportunity grew as well, allowing him to expand his creativity and experiment with what would become industry innovators like full-color three-strip Technicolor, synchronized sound, technical developments with cameras, and feature-length cartoons. Walt was always in search of the latest and greatest, and oftentimes his experimentations with his own personal projects would lead to new things he could bring with him to work. Some of these innovations would change the way that cartoons were made indefinitely. Movies that included these Disney innovations include *Snow White and the Seven Dwarfs*, *Pinocchio*, *Fantasia*, *Dumbo*, and *Bambi*.

After World War II, Walt Disney ventured further into new territory with live-action films like *Mary Poppins*, which won five Academy Awards. The movie itself was satisfying for Walt, who had been fighting to get the rights for the story for years. Its success may be a deciding factor in the future live-action productions that Disney took on in the years after its release.

Those that knew Walt Disney knew him to be a self-deprecating and shy man while in private, despite his outgoing and warm public persona as the father of the Disney film company and Mickey Mouse. His expectations were always set high, both for himself and for the people around him. His desire to make sure everything was perfect led him to be uptight and strict, especially at work, and would lead to him overworking himself and overstressing himself. On at least one occasion, it caused him to take time off from work because he was pushed to exhaustion and a mental breakdown. Despite the stress it caused himself and the employees at his company, he liked the world to see him as the kind, warm father that everyone dreamed of having.

The 1950s held one of the biggest physical expansions in Walt Disney's resume with the creation of the Disney amusement parks. In order to be able to afford this endeavor, he diversified his current interests by stepping into the land of television broadcasted programming with *The Mickey Mouse Club* and *Walt Disney's Disneyland*. By collaborating with ABC and signing a contract with them, he was able to pull in more money from ABC as well as merchandising deals. In an attempt to grow his business, he also took part in planning events such as the 1959 Moscow Fair, the 1960 Winter Olympics, and the 1964 New York World's Fair. By 1955, he was able to open his first park, known as Disneyland.

The second would begin the stages of planning in 1965, under the name Disney World. The golden center of this second amusement park project was meant to be a prototype for a new type of city, and it was called Experimental Prototype Community of Tomorrow, or EPCOT. Walt Disney put a lot of thought and planning into both of his amusement parks, but EPCOT certainly took his time and ideas to a whole new level. His plans for Disney World were going to be epic and beyond comparison, connecting people to the current developments in technology and animation through a futuristic society hosted in a pleasant city within the Disney World park.

Due to smoking heavily throughout his entire life, Walt Disney became ill with little warning and died soon after of lung cancer in 1966. The time in between his diagnosis and his death was incredibly short. Unfortunately, he did not live long enough to see his Disney World amusement park creation come to life and it never reached the glory of his ultimate goals. His brother, Roy Disney, took over the Disney business and chose to go the easier route and bring Disney World to life in a way that kept it similar to the first Disney park known as Disneyland and located in Anaheim, California.

Since his death, there have been accusations that Walt Disney was anti-Semitic and racist. These allegations even go as far as to accuse him of supporting the Nazi party in some of the most extreme gossip, but his family and the people that knew him personally have all denied even the slightest bit of truth to any of these allegations. Not only have family members of the beloved animator stood up in his defense, but former employees as well. When he was alive, he was a provider of family values but since his death, he has been accused more often of being a spokesperson for American intolerance and imperialism. He's also been called a cynical manipulator of simple, common commercial and cultural formulas. This could be due in part to his rigidly strict principles and his high work ethic, but it also due in part to specifically racist content that was considered "okay" at the time certain films were being made. It doesn't help that he has been accused of using his work to rewrite American history in a more favorable, optimistic light. The Walt Disney Family Museum has also acknowledged the fact that there are racial stereotypes immortalized in some of their earlier cartoons. Despite all of the accusations thrown Disney's way, nobody that has ever worked for his company has ever accused him of openly making any anti-Semitic taunts or slurs and there were many Jewish people that worked at the Disney companies under his employ, many of which were given the responsibilities of influential positions within the company that could be used to argue against these allegations. Walt was also a regular donator to a variety of Jewish charities during his life and the B'nai B'rith chapter in Beverly Hills named him their 1955 Man of the Year. After an investigation headed by the first person to be granted full, unrestricted access to Disney's archived files, it was concluded that there was not enough evidence of anti-Semitism to officially condemn Walt Disney as an anti-Semite. Though it was also concluded that even though Walt himself was not an anti-Semite, it is known that he allied himself for a brief period of time with the Motion Picture Alliance for the Preservation of American Ideals, which he distanced himself from in the 1950s, presumably because he was getting to know better what the group was about. Though he did voluntarily step away from this group, he was never quite able to wash the stain of their touch from his reputation.

Regardless of the negative connotations associated with his name since his death, none can deny his importance in film and animation history and in the cultural fabric of the United States. The awards and commendations he has won and been awarded speak for themselves, but so does his work and the innovations he's brought into the future of animation and filmmaking. His movies are still shown, re-released, and adapted quite frequently, and his legacy lives on with Disney as a film company, the Disney amusement parks that now span several countries, and so much more. His high standards and expectations live on in the Disney company's continued efforts in the production of popular entertainment and they inspire other innovators in the field of entertainment, film, television, and animation as well. No matter what your opinion of Walt Disney may be, none can argue against the extraordinary magnitude of the span of contact that his work has had on the world. The physical proof of his existence is everywhere. Walk into any mall, scan the channels on your television on any day, or even just walk out of your house and chances are, something that was created by Disney will cross your path.

The Formative Years - His Early Life (1901-1920)

Born on the 5th of December in 1901, Walter Elias Disney was born into the world in the Hermosa neighborhood in Chicago at the address 1249 Tripp Avenue. Before him, his parents had already bore three children; Herbert, Raymond, and Roy, which made Walt the fourth as well as the youngest son. His father's name was Elias Disney, which is the middle name that he was given came from, and the father was born to two Irish parents in the Province of Canada. His mother's name was Flora, maiden name Call, and she was born to American parents, one of English and one of German descent. In 1903, they'd have their first daughter together and name her Ruth. Despite her being two years younger than him, they both started school at the same time in late 1909.

When Walt was four, the family picked up and moved onto his uncle Robert's newly purchased piece of land in Marceline, Missouri. His first brush with art came after the move, when he was paid by a retired neighborhood doctor to draw the horse they owned at the man's request. To get better at art through the art of practice, Walt would take his father's old copies of the newspaper *Appeal to Reason* and study Ryan Walker's cartoons from the front page so that he could draw copies of them on his own. It was easy to judge his skill and improvement by testing out how close he could get to looking like a legitimate copy-artist. During this time, he also began working with watercolors and crayons and showed proficient talents. It was all about exploration and learning new things.

Living near the Santa Fe Railway line and the Atchison, Topeka also birthed a fascination with trains in general, their mechanics, and the way they worked. He could look at and listen to them almost whenever he wanted, drawing inspiration from them and intrigue from their mechanics. This fascination with trains would follow him into his adult life, and later fuel his decision to have a train installed in his backyard as well as through his first amusement park achievement, Disneyland.

Another move took the Disney family out of the place they had come to know as home and brought them to Kansas City, Missouri in 1911, and this move unknowingly brought

Walt closer to his future and inspiration for his career as well. It was in Kansas City that he met a boy by the name of Walter Pfeiffer, because they attended Benton Grammar school together as students. The Pfeiffer family was incredibly interested in theatre and brought Walt into the world of vaudeville and introduced him to motion pictures. They saw his love for being educated and took to providing him with as much entertainment education as the boy could absorb. Eventually, it got to the point where he was spending more time with the Pfeiffer family than at his own home. He really enjoyed being able to study these new forms of entertainment he'd been introduced to, more than just as something interesting to watch to waste some time before he found something better to do. He liked them as even more than the bits of disposable entertainment that many people used them for.

Because their father, Elias, bought the *Kansas City Times* and *The Kansas City Star*'s newspaper routes, Walt and Roy would get up every morning at 4:30am so that they could deliver the *Times*' morning paper. Later in the day, they'd go out after school so that they could deliver for the route dedicated to the *Star*. The boys were both exhausted by their hectic work schedules and Walt would even fall asleep in class and get in trouble on a consistent basis because of it. Still, they continued to do their part to work for the family for over six years of their own free will, despite it cutting into their sleep. Some believe that the work ethic he held onto so tightly as an adult was born in this time.

He also attended the Kansas City Art Institute during this time and took Saturday courses while attending a corresponding course in cartooning. He wasn't old enough to earn any degrees of any kind, but he wanted the experience and the knowledge these courses brought him. His schedule was already full with school and his paper routes, but he pushed himself so that he could successfully add this to his schedule as well.

The Disney father's ventures in business grew in 1917 when he bought stock in the O-Zell company, a Chicago jelly producer, giving his children another look into the world of business. In the meantime, Walt was expanding his own ventures by joining the school newspaper at McKinley High School as a cartoonist. He drew patriotic panels that were inspired by the first World War, which was happening all around him at the time. At the same time, he continued his art education at the Chicago Academy of Fine Arts by taking night classes. Walt couldn't get enough art in his life and would take every opportunity to put more of it into his life.

His patriotism called him to try to join the United States Army in 1918 so that he could help his country in its fight against Germany, but he didn't reach the age requirement and was rejected. He wasn't eighteen yet, so he was turned away for being too young. Knowing that he was still legally too young to help in the ways that he wanted to, he tried to sate his need to help again in September of the same year by joining the Red Cross, after changing the date on his birth certificate. This attempt was successful, much to his glee. He was then accepted into active service and was then sent to France where he was ordered to serve as an ambulance driver after the armistice was done in November. Always creative at heart, he had a habit of drawing creative cartoons along the outside of the ambulance that he drove. Some would think that an act like that was considered vandalism, but he never met with harsh critics. Instead, his fellow volunteers really enjoyed the work and it lightened the heavy duties they were there to uphold. The lighthearted nature of the aesthetic his art left behind on his ambulance was well received, and it even opened the door for the army newspaper, *Stars and Stripes,* publishing some of his work.

In 1919, Walt came back to the United States and settled back down in Kansas City in the month of October. Pesmen-Rubin Commercial Art Studio hired him on as an apprentice artist almost immediately, where he was tasked with illustrating commercials for advertising purposes, catalogs, and theater programs. It certainly wasn't the dream job for an animator with vast amounts of creativity, but it paid well and put experience on his resume. This is also where he met Ub Iwerks, who would become priceless as far as Walt's friendships and his future are concerned. Not only was Ub Iwerks going to become one of the Walt's friends and a co-worker that would stand by him when all others walked away from him, but he worked side by side with Walt to create the most iconic Disney character in the world, Mickey Mouse. This character would come at the moment that they needed him most, and when they breathed life into him, he breathed life back into Disney Studios. Without Ub Iwerks, Mickey Mouse would not be who he is today and Disney Studios wouldn't be the same either.

The Start Of A Legend - His Early Career (1920-1928)

Though they had greatly enjoyed their time with the company up until this point, Walt and his friend Ub Iwerks were laid off from their jobs at Pesmen-Rubin in January of 1920 after the post-holiday season saw the company's revenue decline. The company could no longer afford to have so many animators on the payroll and they were both new and easily expendable. In response to a need to find new work, they collaborated and put their heads together in the creation of their first joint company, Iwerks-Disney Commercial Artists, though it was short-lived because they had trouble pulling in new customers. It wasn't as easy as it had looked when they had a big name behind them to attract business. Try as they might, they couldn't get enough customer interest in their company to survive and keep their business afloat. The two agreed that the best course of action for the moment was for Walt to leave the company temporarily to take on a more stable job with steady income at the Kansas City Film Ad Company, which was managed by A. V. Cauger. When Ub Iwerks realized that he could not run their company alone and it was still not bringing in enough money to support even just one person, he followed Walt to the Kansas City Film Ad Company in the following months and started working there as well.

While at this company the two worked with the cutout animation technique, which was the company's chosen form of animation.

Though his preferences were towards drawing cartoons, like *Koko the Clown* and *Mutt and Jeff*, his interest in animation was born during this time as well. Borrowing a camera and a book on animation, he took this interest home with him and began experimenting on his own. His opinion, after this experimentation, was that cel animation was the better option to the cutout method he was using at work. The owner of the company, Cauger, would not be persuaded to change the animation method, though Walt did try. Wanting to continue pursuing cel animation, but in a more professional environment with creditable results, he partnered with a co-worker, Fred Harman, and opened up a new company. The local Newman Theater was the biggest client of this new business owned by Walt Disney and Fred Harman, buying and then reselling their short cartoons under the name Newman's Laugh-O-Grams. The first six of these Laugh-O-Grams were fairy tales written with a modern twist, inspired by Walt's interest in Paul Terry's *Aesop's Fables*.

These Laugh-O-Grams were so successful that in May of 1921 a new company was made to house them called Laugh-O-Gram Studio. More animators were hired to assist with the rise in demand for more Laugh-O-Grams, including Ub Iwerks, Rudolf Ising, and Fred Harman's own brother, Hugh. However, there was still not enough money being made by these cartoons to keep the company running, even with the heightened demand, so Walt had to pursue other options as well to keep funding the project.

This other option became a production by the name of *Alice's Wonderland*, which was made with a combination of live action and animation based on *Alice's Adventures in Wonderland*. Virginia Davis was cast as the main character, Alice. The finished project was twelve and a half minutes long in total on one reel of film, but it took too long to finish and could not save Laugh-O-Gram Studio's from going bankrupt in 1923.

On the dawn of another new horizon, in July of 1923 Walt moved to Hollywood. At the time, the cartoon universe's center was New York, but his brother Roy was in Los Angeles, recovering from tuberculosis. His brother attracted more interest than his interest in his career, so he followed his heart to his brother. His career could be fanned no matter what his location was, he had faith in his talents.

Even so, it began to look like he wouldn't be able to see his latest project, *Alice's Wonderland*, until Margaret J. Winkler, a film distributor from New York, contacted him in interest. She was in need of a new series to attach to her name, because she was about to lose the rights to both *Felix the Cat* and *Out of the Inkwell*. A distributor without content to distribute has no income. The contract was signed for six *Alice* comedies, with the possibility for two more, six episode series in the future if *Alice* went well on the table as well. Together with his brother, Roy and Walt worked to fill the order for these cartoons under their new company name,

Disney Brothers Studio. This is the company that would later become The Walt Disney Company and follow their family name into infamy. As production began, they were able to convince Virginia Davis (their star, Alice) to move to Hollywood with her family so that she could continue to be part of the project. Her contract for this time promised her a monthly payment of $100. Ub Iwerks was the next to be convinced to move out to Hollywood to join Walt Disney and company, coming in from Kansas City.

In the early months of 1925, an ink artist had been hired in by the name of Lillian Bounds, and Walt grew close with her quickly. The two of them spent an increasing amount of time together. In July of that year, they were happily married. Lillian was quoted saying that they shared a happy marriage, though it was said by Walt Disney's biographer, Neal Gabler, that he spoke a lot about being henpecked, because his wife spoke her mind when she didn't agree with his decisions or see him as an unquestionable superior. In a household during that era, a wife like that was rare and oftentimes dreaded. Lillian was happy managing the house and supporting her husband as a housewife and had little interest in the intricacies of animation or film. She was equally uninterested in the Hollywood social scene. Together, they had two daughters by the names of Diane and Sharon. Diana was born in December of 1933 while Sharon was adopted six weeks after she was born in December of 1936. They did not hide their adoption and were open about it with family, but did not like when anyone outside of their family brought it up. They didn't want to hide the adoption from either of their daughters or their family, but they didn't think it was anyone else's business. In general, they kept their daughter's lives as private as possible, even going as far as to make sure that the press never got their photographs. They didn't want to share their children with the public, especially after the Lindbergh kidnapping.

Margaret J. Winkler had given her distribution role in the *Alice* series to her husband by 1926, but there were occasional problems between him and Walt. These problems only escalated after the deal for *Alice* was done and new negotiations needed to be made. They continued running the series until July of 1927, at which point Walt was mentally done with the project and Mintz and was more than ready to move on from it and the mixed format. Looking to create something completely different, Walt partnered with Ub Iwerks again and made the character Oswald the Lucky Rabbit come to life in reply to Winkler's husband, Charles Mintz, asking them to send him new content so that it could be distributed through Universal Pictures. Walt's intentions for the character were to keep him "peppy, alert, saucy and venturesome, keeping him also neat and trim." An attempt to negotiate a higher fee for the *Oswald* series by Walt revealed that Charles Mintz was actually interested in lowering the prices. Mintz also spoke with some of Walt's artists at this time and talked them into working directly for him instead of Walt, effectively stealing them right out from underneath him. It also came to light that legally, Universal owned his

Oswald character because they held the intellectual property rights. With the upper hand in his corner, Mintz told Walt that he would create a new animation studio with the employees he now had working under him and make the series without Walt if he didn't accept the price reductions. Walt did not accept the threat and refused the ultimatum, which cost him the majority of his animation crew. Iwerks was the only artist to stay on Disney's team after he left Mintz.

Mickey Mouse Is Born – The Academy Awards (1928-1933)

With the loss of their new character Oswald, Walt and Ub Iwerks were in need of a new character to market and write about. Together, they created Mickey Mouse in the hopes that he would be that new character. It's rumored that a mouse Walt had owned as a pet during their earlier Laugh-O-Gram days was the inspiration for the character, though there is no real confirmation on how Mickey's concept was actually born. It is known, however, that the first name Walt used for the character was Mortimer Mouse, but his wife Lillian convinced him that it sounded too uptight and in her constructive criticism, gave the name Mickey as an alternative that he picked up and used instead. Walt's concept art for the character was then revised by Iwerks so that it would be simpler to take the character and make an animation out of him. Walt himself provided Mickey's voice once his physical appearance was settled, and he continued to do so until 1947. Originally, this decision was made due to a lack of budget, but it was one of the best choices Disney ever made. When asked to describe the birth of this iconic cartoon character, one employee under Disney later said, "Ub designed Mickey's physical appearance, but Walt gave him his soul."

The first official appearance of Mickey Mouse was in a single test screening in May of 1928, in a short titled *Plane Crazy*. The second time Mickey Mouse appeared on film was in *Gallopin' Gaucho*, and neither cartoons caught enough attention to be sold to a distributor. Taking inspiration from the success of *The Jazz Singer* in 1927, Walt decided later that his next experiment would be synchronized sound and he used it on his third Mickey Mouse film, *Steamboat Willie*, making the world's official first cartoon with sound. Upon completion, Pat Powers, the former executive of Universal Pictures, signed a contract with Walt that required he make use of the Powers Cinephone with his animations as a recording system. The sound from Disney's early cartoons all rely on Powers as their new distributor, which quickly became the industry's popular choice.

Always looking to make his work better, Walt looked to a professional arranger and composer by the name of Carl Stalling to improve his cartoons by adding his input to the musical choices. This choice paid off almost immediately with the series *Silly Symphonies* being born based on Carl's suggestions. Several other local artists were also added to the production company's staff, some of which became the first of the first artists to stay with Disney as core animators in later years, when the studio was more popular and being part of it was actually worth something. During this time, the animation production group was called the Nine Old Men and their initial success came from both their work on Mickey Mouse and *Silly Symphonies*.

Despite their commercial success, both Disney brothers were unhappy with Powers and felt they weren't getting the share of the profits that they deserved. Ub Iwerks had been taking the responsibility of animating each cel of animation on his own, which put a lot of time on one of the higher paying animation experts, and in 1930, Walt tried to get him to cut down on the work he was doing by allowing some of the lower-paid employees to take care of some of the more tedious and simple animation frames by drawing only the key poses himself as guidelines. Still, Walt approached Powers about being given a raise for the success of his cartoons in the hopes that he'd be able to pay himself and his staff the wages that they deserved, but attempts to negotiate were refused and Powers signed only Iwerks to his team instead. Not only did that mean that Walt lost, in a sense, but the consensus both in the animation world and at the studio was that the Disney Studio was destined to close without Iwerks on the team.

At this point in his life, this is where Walt Disney's social problems really began to put stress on his relationships with the people that held up his career. Many former employees of the Disney Studio have been quoted on record saying that Walt was often cold and seemed incapable of giving them motivation or praise. "That'll work" was considered high praise from him, possibly based on his incredibly high standards and how difficult it was to actually impress him. Incentive didn't come in the form of flattering words, it came in the shape of monetary bonuses or career-building recommendations, and he expected his staff to get the memo without the praise having to be spoken out loud.

In October of 1931, the amount of stress that he was under caused Walt to slide into a nervous breakdown. Personally, he attributed his failing mental state to the fact that he was constantly overworking himself as well as the inner machinations of the trouble between himself, the loss of Iwerks, and the irritation that was Powers. In order to regain his health and some peace of mind, he took his wife Lillian on a cruise to Panama and another cruise to Cuba for an extended holiday to get away from it all. He wanted to indulge in family life, rest, and leave the troubles of being a budding animation tycoon at the office.

The subject of Walt Disney's personality and what kind of person he really was has been up for debate multiple times, both before and after his death. The public persona that he shared with the world painted him as someone that was much different than his actual personality. According to his biographer, the concept of intentionally hiding behind the public personality he'd created for himself was a way to become something greater and more confident than the anxieties of a small man in the middle of the big universe. Others argue that the bashful tycoon that was marketed to us was just that; a marketing ploy, and he knew that he was acting, and he knew just what his acting would do to the adoring public around him. It's no wonder that a public personality was created, with critics commenting on his private attitude and naming that version of him as common and every day. Walt himself has been quoted acknowledging the fact that there are two different sides to him, saying, "I'm not Walt Disney. I do a lot of things Walt Disney would not do. Walt Disney does not smoke. I smoke. Walt Disney does not drink. I drink." It is clear that regardless of how much of his fabricated personality was fake and false, he created it to better suit his needs as the head of Disney.

Now in need of a new distributor after his trouble with Powers, Walt took Disney Studio to Columbia Pictures and signed a contract that would put Mickey Mouse cartoons in distribution again. These cartoons became incredibly popular, growing to become an international demand.

Always interested by new technology, in 1932 Walt shot *Flowers and Trees* in full-color three-strip Technicolor. This project won in audience popularity, and even won the Best Short Subject (Cartoon) award at the 1932 Academy Awards. At the same ceremony, he was given an Honorary Award for the creation of the character Mickey Mouse. As a bonus to the success of *Flowers and Trees* and its new media development, he managed to also negotiate his way through a deal that allowed him the ownership and sole right to continue to make use of this three-strip process until the 31st of August in 1935. After that, he made use of color in all of his following *Silly Symphony* cartoons.

The year 1933 saw another Walt Disney success with the production *The Three Little Pigs*. Adrian Danks, a media historian, later said that the film was, "the most successful short animation of all time." As if to prove that opinion, another Academy Award was given to Walt for Short Subject (cartoon) and because of the amount of success the cartoon received, the studio was able to increase the amount of people that were on the staff payroll. By the end of the year, Disney had almost two hundred people working for him. At this time he was also able to expand the skill types of people he employed and the way he used them to better his films by creating a story department that was completely separate from their current staff of animators. This story department was there to help Walt ensure that he did not lose his audience and his work told stories that were emotionally gripping. Together, they plotted out storylines through storyboards and picked apart the creativity and the content behind new projects and made sure that the base concepts were the best that they could be before they were fleshed out as full films or shorts.

Full Steam Success – The Golden Age Of Animation (1934-1941)

By the year 1943, Walt found that he couldn't find the same satisfaction in making short, formulaic cartoons as he had in his earlier years of animation. He'd been making them for so long that they felt stale, and he wanted to try something new; something bigger. He was no longer satisfied with the way he'd been animating or the content he'd been putting into those animations. He needed something big to funnel his attention into, something with meaning and a real impact. His next production would span four years, and at the end of that time he would produce the feature-length animated film, *Snow White and the Seven Dwarfs*. News of Walt's intention was leaked before the project was complete and many people speculated that a project of that size would end Disney's company in bankruptcy and it earned the nickname Disney's Folly because of it. By the end, the film cost the studio $1.5 million to make, which was three times more than the budget that had been passed. But despite the premature critics and despite going so far over budget, the film was also the first full color and sound animated feature and Walt's need for the best put his animators in the Chouinard Art Institute to take courses to improve the realism in their animation before they finished working on the film. He also had actors and live animals brought into the studio to give his animators models to study as they worked. He was determined to make this film a success and to teach his employees something new while he was at it.

Snow White is also responsible for Disney's making his presence known in the Asia Pacific. The first screening of the film in the 1930s was in Shanghai. In 2016, Disney Parks and Resorts would open the Shanghai Disneyland Resort, which saw over 10 million people walk through it in the first year alone.

Further technical innovations were brought to the table with the creation of the multiplane camera and the technique that went along with it that allowed the animators to layer their drawings on different pieces of glass so that they could be moved independently and set at different distances to create depth. The background could be drawn out on one piece of glass, which one of the main characters on another, separate piece. A third piece could be used for incidental scenery pieces that move during the animation. When all three pieces were moved, it added a sense of depth and allowed pieces to be moved independently. These glass pieces were moved in order to make the effect of a camera panning across a scene look more realistic. The first time Disney used this technique was for a *Silly Symphony* cartoon by the title *The Old Mill* in 1937, which later won for Best Animated Short Film at the Academy Awards because it was just so visually impressive. By the time the multiplane camera technology was ready to be put to use, the *Snow White and the Seven Dwarfs* project was almost already done, so Walt had some of the scenes redrawn in the new multiplane format because he knew that they would look better if they took the extra time to redo them.

In December of 1937, the full-length feature film made its debut and received positive reviews and praise from both the audience and film critics. *Snow White* earned the title of most successful motion picture of 1938, as well as most successful sound film at the time, with a total of $6.5 million gross by May of 1939. Another Honorary Academy Award was given to Disney, and in honor of *Snow White and the Seven Dwarfs*, the award that was given to him was one full-size Oscar with seven miniature statuettes. Because of the success that came out of *Snow White*, Disney Studio championed one of the most productive periods of time within the company. This time is known as the Golden

Age of Animation by the Walt Disney Family Museum.

Now that *Snow White* was finished, Disney moved towards its next project. In early 1928, *Pinocchio* began production and November brought *Fantasia*, ready to begin production as well. In 1940, both animated feature films were released to the public, though both were rather unsuccessful with the box office. Part of that was due to World War II causing revenues to drop the year before in 1939. The studio had no choice but to take their losses on both projects, and by the end of February of 1941 Disney had fallen into deep debt.

In order to turn their financial crisis around and make some money, Walt and his brother Roy opened up the first public stock offering for the Disney company in 1940 and had to cut their staff's wages heavily. This drop in salary for the Disney staff, coupled with Walt's habit of handling staff in an insensitive and high-handed manner, caused the animators to strike in 1941. This strike lasted a total of five weeks and caused the National Labor Relations Board to send down a federal mediator to negotiate and speak with both sides. Knowing that there was no way to end this conflict that would be fully positive for Disney Studio, Walt planned a goodwill trip to South America after taking an offer that was given to him by the Office of the Coordinator of Inter-American Affairs. The strike, coupled with the company's financial crisis, gave several animators enough reason to leave the studio and left some of those that had stayed with an indefinite strain on their relationship with Disney.

The strike was also responsible for delaying production of Disney's next project, Dumbo. The film itself was made inexpensively in a simple manner and was released in 1941 to positive reviews from critics as well as the audience.

The Second World War And Moving Forward (1941-1950)

The United States stood up to take its place in World War II in 1941 ,soon after *Dumbo* was released in October. Putting his cartooning skill to a productive use that was relevant to the needs of his country's troops, Walt created a group within his company called the Walt Disney Training Films Unit and tasked the animators to create instructional films like *Aircraft Production Methods* and *Four Methods of Flush Riveting* for use in the military. He added to his contributions to his country by agreeing to use his character Donald Duck for short cartoons meant to promote the sale of war bonds after he met with the Secretary of the Treasury, Henry Morgenthau Jr. In addition, Disney is responsible for propaganda productions like *Der Fuehrer's Face* and a feature film in 1943 by the name of *Victory Through Air Power*.

None of the films that Disney made for the military earned the company enough money to do anything but cover the cost of production. In April of 1942, *Bambi* was released and didn't do as well as Disney had hoped, at the box office it lost $200,000. In addition, *Fantasia* and *Pinocchio* had brought in low earnings, leaving Disney $4 million in debt in 1944 on an agreement with Bank of America. Because of this debt, the bank basically held the future of Disney's company in their hands, and held a meeting to discuss what they would do about the debt. Amadeo Giannini, the founder and chairman, was quoted telling his executives, "I've been watching the Disneys' pictures quite closely because I knew we were lending them money far above the financial risk. … They're good this year, they're good next year, and they're good the year after. … You have to relax and give them time to market their product."

Despite that level of confidence, Disney slowed and made less short films in the years of the late 1940s. Metro-Goldwyn-Mayer and Warner Bros. were emerging as stiff competition in the field of animation. Because of their financial struggles, Roy Disney brought the idea of combining live-action and animation work to the table again. Taking this suggestion, a series of live-action films were initiated in 1948. These popular nature films were called *True-Life Adventures* and the first in the series, *Seal Island*, won the Best Short Subject (Two-Reel) at the Academy Awards.

As Walt Disney grew older, he became more conservative with politics. His support for the Democratic Party remained firm until he switched to the Republican Party during the 1940 presidential election in order to support and donate to Thomas E. Dewey's bid for the 1944 presidency. He was one of the founders of the Motion Picture Alliance for the Preservation of American Ideals in 1946. The ideals of the organization were that they, "believed in, and like, the American Way of Life. … We find ourselves in sharp revolt against a rising tide of Communism, Fascism and kindred beliefs that seek by subversive means to undermine a change this way of life." The House Un-American Activities Committee (HUAC) brought Walt before them during the Second Red Scare, and in his testimony he branded William Pomerance, David Hilberman, and Herbert Sorrell as communist agitators. These men had formerly worked beneath Disney as animators and he called their part in the strike against his company in 1941 an organized effort to gain communist influence over Hollywood.

Walt took his family and moved again in 1949, bringing them to Holmby Hills district in Los Angeles to find their new home. His friends Betty and Ward Kimball had a railroad in their backyard, and Walt got their help in having blueprints made so that he could have a miniature live steam railroad built in his own backyard. He called this the

Carolwood Pacific Railroad, because Carolwood Drive was the street their home was located on. An engineer from Disney Studios was responsible for building this locomotive, Roger E. Broggie. The train itself was named Lilly Belle after his wife and remained in use on his property for three years before he had it sent to storage after his guests were involved in multiple accidents on it.

New Media – Amusement Parks, Television, And Expanded Interests (1950-1966)

After eight years without an animated feature, Disney released *Cinderella* in the early 1950s. Walt and the employees at his company were happy when it was a success, receiving good reviews from the audience and critics alike. It cost the studio $2.2 million to make and made almost $8 million within just the first year. During the production of the film, Walt himself was preoccupied with *Treasure Island*, so he wasn't as involved with *Cinderella* as he had been with the projects that had come before it. *The Story of Robin Hood and His Merrie Men* was released in 1952, and Disney put his time into more live-action films, with a common theme of patriotism. Though he wasn't done with his full-length animations either, and he finished *Alice In Wonderland* in 1951 and *Peter Pan* in 1953, Walt put more of his own attention into other things. So much of the animation was left to his animation department that they ran most of their operations on their own, though he did attend all meetings that brought new stories to the table.

The first of these personal ventures for Walt went back to something that he had been thinking about for several years; a themed amusement park. He had taken his daughters to Griffith Park in Los Angeles, and he had made a visit to Copenhagen,

Denmark to see the Tivoli Gardens. He desired an unspoiled park that was clean and could entertain children and their parents and was influenced by these visits with his children. Zoning permission came in March of 1952, allowing him to erect an amusement park near the Disney studios in Burbank. After some research, Walt decided that the plot he had been looking at was too small and he decided instead to purchase a larger plot thirty-five miles south of the studio in Anaheim.

The downfall of the bigger plot was that it was further away from the studio, which might cause a wrinkle in his plan by giving shareholders something to complain about. To rectify this potential danger, Walt decided to make the project more personal by distancing it from Disney Studios, funding it with his own money and hiring a team outside of Disney Studios to work on the planning process for the theme park. This team became known as Imagineers, and in mid-1954 the Imagineers were tasked with visiting other amusement parks around the globe and taking notes, so that Disney could see what he could learn from the competition. Bank funding came in for this theme park project, so he invited other stockholders, Western Printing and Lithographing Company, and American Broadcasting-Paramount Theatres to get their feet in the door as well by putting their money in too. Official construction began in July of 1954 and Disneyland opened its doors for the first time a year later in July of 1955. ABC broadcast the opening ceremony and 70 million viewers tuned in to watch it.

The design for the park split it up into various themed sections, all brought together by Main Street, U.S.A. a replica of a street in Marceline, Walt's hometown. The various themes for the different parts of the park were Frontierland, Adventureland, Tomorrowland, and Fantasyland. Another big feature in the park was Disneyland Railroad, a train that's track also linked all of the different parts of the park. The walls to the park were intentionally built to be tall, blocking all view of the outside world in this fantastical amusement park. As expected, there were a few small problems with parts of the park during its early months, and it was a huge success. After being open for just a month, Disneyland had seen over 20,000 people a day and that number raised to 2.6 million after its first year.

All of the money that Disney earned through ABC was based on their Disney television programming. Christmas Day in 1950, the studio took part in a television special that revealed some of the behind-the-scenes work that went into making *Alice in Wonderland* and the show was so successful that Roy Disney suspected it would raise their box office debuts by millions. He wrote to shareholders in a letter in March of 1951 saying, "television can be a most powerful selling aid for us, as well as a source of revenue. It will probably be on this premise that we enter television when we do."

After all of the funding for Disneyland had been settled, ABC hosted an anthology made of a combination of live-action features, animations, and other content in 1954 called *Walt Disney's Disneyland*. One of the segments featured on *Disneyland* was a miniseries with five parts by the name of Davy Crockett. Records with the theme song, *The Ballad of Davy Crockett*, sold ten million records internationally and inspired Walt Disney to create a company to produce and distribute records that he called Disneyland Records. The ratings for the show were successful and their audience share was more than 50%, which pleased everyone involved and made the television special the beginning of further collaborations. The Mickey Mouse Club was born, becoming the first daily television show with the Disney name on it. It was a children's variety show and it opened up further opportunities for collaborations between Disney and his company. For example, Western Printing became a business associate when it began producing merchandise for the show.

Disneyland wasn't the only project that took Walt outside of the animation center within Disney Studio. In 1959, he was named a consultant for the American National Exhibition in Moscow. His contribution, a nineteen-minute long feature that includes 360-degree Circarama theater called *America the Beautiful*, was credited to Disney Studios and became one of the most liked attractions. In 1960, his name was connected to the Winter Olympics when he was given the role of chairman of the Pageantry Committee and was put in charge of orchestrating the medal, opening, and closing ceremonies.

Walt didn't let his work outside of Disney Studios distract him from his television and film work either. In an episode of the *Disneyland* series titled *Man in Space,* Walt collaborated with rocket designer from NASA, Wernher von Braun. He also made a return to the studios to manage parts of the production for *Lady and the Tramp* in 1955 and *Sleeping Beauty* in 1959, both full-length features. The former was the first time CinemaScope had been used in an animated film and the latter was the first to use Technirama 70 mm film. He returned to the studios again in 1961 for *One Hundred and One Dalmatians*, which was the first time Xerox cels had been used in an animated feature film and again in 1963 for *The Sword in the Stone*.

Walt Disney was invited to leave his symbolic mark on Hollywood in February of 1960 when he was given two stars on the iconic walkway. One star was for his work in television and the other for his work in motion pictures. Mickey Mouse was later given his own star in 1978 for his appearance in motion pictures.

As another change in direction, *Mary Poppins* was produced by Disney in 1964, and was based on a series of books written by the author P.L. Travers. Walt had been after the rights to distribute this story since the 1940s and was to become the most successful film for the Disney company in the 1960s. Travers, however, was not a fan and was quoted afterward saying that he regretted selling the rights to the story.

In the same year, Walt was recruited to help the California Institute of the Arts expand their campus and he worked with an architect to have blueprints drawn up so that a whole new building could be built for the school.

As a participant in the 1964 New York World's Fair, Disney had four exhibits that were made possible by the funding of corporate sponsors that he selected. His step into philanthropy and humanitarianism took place when he created It's a Small World for PepsiCo for their planned tribute to UNICEF. It's a Small World is a boat ride where the patrons are taken through the nations of the world and introduced to audio-animatronic dolls that share imagery of children from around the world. Another ride by the name of Great Moments with Mr. Lincoln featured an animatronic resembling Abraham Lincoln, quoting parts of the former president's speeches. Electricity was promoted with the Carousel of Progress, while mankind's progress was highlighted at Ford's Magic Skyway. These four exhibits were later brought to Disneyland, with It's a Small World remaining the most like the original.

Plans were made in the early to mid-1960s by Walt to use a glacial valley in Mineral King to create a ski resort to add to his name's legacy. Experts such as prestigious as Willy Schaeffler, a well-known Olympic ski couch, were signed on to help design to ski area. Using money that had been made by Disneyland, Walt didn't stop looking for new places that might support another themed amusement park. He finally found what he was looking for a short distance southwest of Orlando, Florida and officially announced that he would develop a new themed amusement park there that would be known as Disney World. A big part of the concept of Disney World was a segment called Magic Kingdom, which was basically a more elaborate, larger version of what Disneyland was, with the addition of resort hotels and golf courses. The heart and center of Disney World was called the Experimental Prototype Community of Tomorrow, or EPCOT. The official description of EPCOT by Walt Disney himself was, "an experimental prototype community of tomorrow that will take its cue from the new ideas and new technologies that are now emerging from the creative centers of American industry. It will be a community of tomorrow that will never be completed, but will always be introducing and testing and demonstrating new materials and systems.

And EPCOT will always be a showcase to the world for the ingenuity and imagination of American free enterprise."

In the year 1966, Walt put his time into helping businesses that would want to sponsor EPCOT once they were successful enough to do so. He also stepped back into the animation studio and put more time into working with his employees on the films attached to his name. During this time, he spent a lot of time with the story development team for *The Jungle Book* and *The Happiest Millionaire*, both were released in 1967. He was also heavily involved in the production of *Winnie the Pooh and the Blustery Day*, a short animated film.

Walt's Failing Health, Cancer, Death, And Beyond (1966 - onward)

During Walt Disney's youth, advertisements and popular media told the world that cigarettes were a beautiful, cool, handsome, and attractive habit that would bring them friendship, love, and sex. Not surprisingly, Walt Disney was one of the many people who fell victim to the siren call of the "cool" cigarette. He smoked non-filtered cigarettes as well as smoking tobacco from a pipe, and the first World War saw him smoking heavily every day. It was not uncommon to see a lit cigarette in the hands of Walt Disney, and he is seen in many photographs with one between his index and middle finger.

In November of 1966, a diagnosis of lung cancer was given and cobalt therapy was initiated in the hopes of treating it. He started to feel sick on November 30th of the same year, causing him to be brought to St. Joseph Hospital for medical care. Ten days after his 65th birthday, on the 15th of December, he suffered a circulatory collapse that was brought on by the lung cancer and summarily passed away. Two days later, his body was cremated and brought to rest in Glendale, California at the Forest Lawn Memorial Park. The whole ordeal from the beginning of the cancer diagnosis to the moment his remains were put to rest was incredibly short and it came incredibly fast.

At the time of his death, his estate held ownership of a holding of 14% in Walt Disney Productions at an estimated total worth of $20 million. In his will, his wife and children were given 45% of his estate through a majority of family trust. 10% of his estate went to his sister, and her children- his nieces and nephews. That left 45% of his estate, which was put in a charitable trust. This charitable trust was designated so that 95% of it went to the California Institute of the Arts with the intention of allowing them to build a better campus, which was an estimated donation of about $15 million. In addition, thirty-eight acres of his land in Valencia at the Golden Oaks ranch was donated to the same school. In 1971, the university was able to move its campus there thanks to Walt Disney's donations.

When *The Happiest Millionaire* and *The Jungle Book* were released in 1967, they brought the total of feature films that Walt Disney had worked on personally up to eighty-one. In 1968, *Winnie the Pooh and the Blustery Day* won an Academy Award for the category of the Short Subject (Cartoon) that was awarded to the Disney company after Walt's death.

Though Walt had grand plans for his fantastical, futuristic society in EPCOT, they were not brought to life. After his death, his brother Roy stepped out of retirement in order to take his brother's place as head of the Disney companies. Construction continued on Disneyland as a project, but in the end Roy decided to change the focus from a functional city like Walt wanted and made it a simple attraction, like Disneyland.

In 1971 at the inauguration, Walt Disney World was dedicated to Walt Disney by his brother Roy. Epcot Center opened in 1982, making Walt Disney World even bigger. The Walt Disney Family Museum was created by one of Walt and Lillian's daughters, Diane, in harmony with her brother, Walter E. D. Miller and opened in 2009 in the Presidio of San Francisco. On display at this museum are thousands of items that held personal significance to Walt Disney and were part of his daily life. Some of his awards are hosted there as well, on display.

Among the awards won by the infamous man known to the world as Walt Disney are fifty-nine Academy Award nominations and twenty-two actual wins, both of which are records held by Disney. He was also nominated for Golden Globe Awards three times, and was presented with two Special Achievement Awards; one in 1942 for *Bambi* and the other in 1953 for *The Living Desert*. As a four-time Emmy Award nominee, he took home one Emmy win in his lifetime for Best Producer on the television series, *Disneyland*. He also won the Cecil B. DeMille Award. The National Film Registry, which is an immortalized collection of "culturally, historically, or aesthetically significant" US films, has inducted *Steamboat Willie, The Three Little Pigs, Snow White and the Seven Dwarfs, Fantasia, Pinocchio, Bambi,* and *Mary Poppins* into its highly selective catalog. According to the American Film Institute's list of 100 greatest American films in 1998, *Snow White and the Seven Dwarfs* ranks at number 49 and *Fantasia* has a place at 58.

Outside of the awards won for his work, in 1935 the French *Legion d'honneur* gave Walt Disney the title of Chevalier. Later in 1952, the country gave him their highest artistic decoration when they awarded him the *Officer d'Academie*. He also received the Order of the Crown from Thailand, the Order of the Southern Cross from Brazil, and the Order of the Aztec Eagle from Mexico. The Presidential Medal of Freedom was given to him on September 14th in 1964, in the United States. He was given the Congressional Gold Medal in 1969, posthumously. The Showman of the World Award was also given to him by the National Association of Theatre Owners. The National Audubon Society gave him their highest honor in 1955, the Audubon Medal, earned through his promotion of the "appreciate and understanding of nature" with his nature films in the *True-Life Adventures*. To add to his list of achievements, Harvard, Yale, the University of California, Los Angeles, and the University of Southern California have all given him honorary degrees.

The records hosted at The Walt Disney Family Museum state that together, all of the members of the Disney family together have won more than 950 honors and special mentions total across the globe. Walt Disney's achievements have literally become out of this world, after an astronomer Lyudmila Karachkina discovered a small planet in 1980 and named it 4017 Disney.

By the year 2014, an estimated 134 million people have come through the Disney themed amusement parks, hosted all over the world. Walt Disney himself has been recast by different actors in many different fictional and biographical works. *The Holy Terror*, a 1938 novel written by H. G. Wells, Walt is referenced. Len Carlou portrayed Walt Disney in a film that debuted on television called *A Dream Is a Wish Your Heart Makes: The Annette Funicello Story* in 1995. Later, Tom Hands played him in *Saving Mr. Banks* in 2013. He was even immortalized in a book with an English-translated titled of *The King of America*, written by Peter Stephan Jungk, a German author. This book is a work of fiction, casting Walt Disney as power-hungry and racist in his later years. The book was later adapted for the opera by composer Philip Glass in 2013 for *The Perfect American.a*

Those wondering how someone with a name in family-friendly entertainment like Walt Disney could be accused of such terrible things, can look to Disney's earlier work for their answers. Some of the productions released between the 1930s and the 1950s exploit racially sensitive material and promote racist imagery. A prime example is the feature film titled Song of the South, which the National Association for the Advancement of Colored People criticized for the way that it obviously perpetuates harmful stereotypes of black people. The film's star, James Baskett, later won an Honorary Academy Award as the first black actor after Walt advocated for his win through the creation of a full-blown campaign. The studio's first black animator, Floyd Norman, has also spoken on Walt

Disney's behalf, stating that, "not once did I observe a hint of the racist behavior Walt Disney was often accused of after his death. His treatment of people—and by this I mean all people—can only be called exemplary."

The consensus of most is that Walt Disney was not actively racist in a way that was meant to be harmful towards anyone else, but just like most everyone in the time period that he grew up during, he was definitely insensitive to racial topics. Still, there are many that don't believe he's so innocent. The harmless way that his cartoons present themselves to children is seen as dangerous by some, because it presents imperialist values as fun that is meant to be consumed by children while others say that even if the cartoons do teach the wrong lessons, that watching them does not have a pedagogic effect.

In direct comparison to these scathing negative reviews, The Times wrote in Walt Disney's obituary, calling his films "wholesome, warm-hearted and entertaining. … of incomparable artistry and of touching beauty."

Langer wrote in the *American Dictionary of National Biography*, "Disney remains the central figure in the history of animation. Through technological innovations and alliances with governments and corporations, he transformed a minor studio in a marginal form of communication into a multinational leisure industry giant. Despite his critics, his vision of a modern corporate utopia as an extension of traditional

American values has possibly gained greater currency in the years after his death."

Live-action films became the main focal point for Disney Studios after the death of Walt Disney until sometime in the late 1980s, at which time Disney Studios entered what *The New York Times* dubbed the Disney Renaissance. This era for the company began with The Little Mermaid in 1989. To this day, Disney's companies are still producing television, film, and stage productions that mirror the successes of Walt's lifetime and continue to work their hardest to live up to his name by producing quality content that is both relevant to the times and newly innovative.

The Television Hall of Fame inducted Walt Disney into their prestigious ranks in 1986.

Following suit in 2006, the California Hall of Fame added him to their ranks as well. 2014 saw another honor for Walt Disney when he was given a star on the Anaheim walk of stars as an inaugural recipient. Among the many things Walt has been known for, he's been called the Pied Piper of Hollywood, a folk-hero, a highly ingenious merchandiser, and he's been credited with forever reshaping culture and the consciousness of the American mind and inspiring us to continue learning and evolving mentally.

The Walt Disney Company (present)

Born as a small, humble business between friends in the 1920s, The Walt Disney Company proudly lives up to the standards of excellence set before it by its founding father. Unquestionably, Walt Disney's legacy was most completely placed under the umbrella of The Walt Disney Company. The mission statement and goal of his company is to continue to remain a leader in the industry of producing and bringing information and entertainment to the world. Their mission statement also pushes them to create content that is of the most innovative, creative, and profitable. The content produced by this company is split into a variety of smaller brands, allowing their services, content, and consumer products to be more organized. This content includes movies, television shows, amusement parks, merchandise, and various other entertainment experiences. As always, the goal is to continue the Disney legacy by bringing world-class experiences and stories to the world that can be enjoyed by the whole family.

In order to maintain that family-friendly experience, Disney has what they call citizenship reports, where the company is given yearly reports based on how closely they are following the company's goals to continue to provide quality and entertaining content. A responsibility supply chain has also become part of the company's operations. Sourcing Disney-branded products ethically is important to the company and a big part of the corporate citizenship efforts. The Walt Disney Company promotes the production of the anything with the Disney name on it by focusing on the improvement of labor conditions at their mass-producing factories, safety testing all products, and continuing to look for new ways to reduce Disney's footprint on the environment.

The Walt Disney Company has been heralded as one of *Fortune*'s World's Most Admired Companies. *Profiles in Diversity Journal* named him a leader in diversity by awarding him the Diversity Award in 2015. The company also received the Edward R. Murrows Award in 2015.

The Walt Disney Company has many affiliates and subsidiary companies, and together they lead in media enterprise and diversified international family entertainment with their parks and resorts, their media networks, their consumer products, their interactive media, and their media networks. These media networks span the use of cable, broadcast, radio, digital, and publishing businesses through ESPN Inc. and the Disney/ABC Television Group. Some of the names under their ownership are the Disney Channel, ABC, and FreeForm.

As the world's largest media company, the leadership behind Disney are responsible for some of the most beloved and well respected brands on the planet. The goal of the strategic direction of The Walt Disney Company is aimed at making the best and the most creative content imaginable, while using the latest technology in their work to nurture innovation. Every day, The Walt Disney Company expands in new worldwide markets. Their diverse team of executives and the members of the Board of Directors keep Disney at the top without sacrificing the values Walt Disney put into the company's creation.

Merchandising may be one of The Walt Disney Company's most diversified assets, ranging through various apps, toys, books, games, clothing, and more. The name for the division in charge or merchandise is called the Disney Consumer Products and Interactive Media, and they're responsible for taking the characters that the animators have brought to life and turning them into digital experiences and physical products meant to continue the adventure and inspire the hearts and minds of those who come in contact with them.

The addition of parks and resorts was of great importance to Walt Disney himself, so it is no wonder that they have continued to expand and grow, remaining a top priority for The Walt Disney Company. These amusement parks and luxury resorts are handled under the company name Walt Disney Parks and Resorts, and this company has become one of the leading providers worldwide when it comes to leisure experiences and family travel. Every year, millions of guests get to experience the vacation of a lifetime at the many Disney parks and resorts. They are infamously known as places that people can make memories that will last their whole life. For this reason, many people propose at Disney locations, and others bring their wedding parties there. The locations under the title of Walt Disney Parks and Resorts include the Disneyland Resort, Walt Disney World, and the Shanghai Disney Resort as well as many more.

The birth of The Walt Disney Company came in the field of animation, and its predecessor, Disney Studios, was where it all began. The studio is one of the most important parts of the company and they continue to give the world quality music, movies, and stage productions across the world. Today, their animation studios include Walt Disney Animation Studios and Pixar Animation Studios.

In Japan, Disney owns and runs the Tokyo Disney Resort on top of a range of diverse businesses that range from studio entertainment and media networks to interactive media and consumer products. The presence of The Walt Disney Company appears in Shanghai as well, with their Shanghai Disneyland Resort. In the Middle East, Africa, and Europe, The Walt Disney Company has led in excellence for their family entertainment for over eighty years. Latin America has also received the Disney businesses and brands right in their own homes in the form of digital and on-air entertainment, music, consumer products, animation, theatrical productions, and live-action publications.

Globally, people have fallen in love with Disney characters and the content produced by The Walt Disney Company for ninety years. Across the world, people are familiar with the stories, experiences, and characters of Disney. Guests come to visit the parks from all over the world, and their movies, radio shows, and television shows are distributed worldwide in a variety of languages. The company itself has operations based in over forty countries across the globe and the actors cast in roles that would immortalize them forever and the employees that keep it running world together to produce experiences in entertainment that are loved and cherished both locally and internationally.

Made in the USA
Lexington, KY
21 August 2019